Siege and Symphony

Myra Schneider

Second Light Publications

For Planet Earth

All profits from the sale of this book will
go to The Woodland Trust

Siege and Symphony

First published 2021 by
Second Light Publications
3 Springfield Close
East Preston
West Sussex
BN16 2SZ

e-mail: info@secondlightlive.co.uk
website: www.secondlightlive.co.uk
ISBN 978-0-9927088-4-9

Printed and bound by Catford Print Centre, PO Box 563, London, SE6 4PY
Cover artwork by Martin Parker at silbercow.co.uk
Typeface Minion font series

Acknowledgements

Credit is due to the following publications where some of these poems, or earlier versions of them, first appeared:

Acumen, Agenda, ARTEMISpoetry, Domestic Cherry, Dreamcatcher, Envoi, Frogmore Papers, Hearing Voices, The High Window, anthology *Locked Down* (Poetry Space 2021), *The London Grip,* anthology *Lovely, Dark and Deep* (Grey Hen Press 2021), *Marble Poetry, Pennine Platform, POEM, Poetry & All that Jazz, Poetry Salzburg, Raceme, Quadrant,* anthology *A Scream of Many Colours: Poems for Now* (Poetry Space 2019), *Stand.*

Cropthorne Church was first published in *What Women Want* (Second Light Publications 2012), and *The Real Mrs Beeton* in *Persephone in Finsbury Park* (Second Light Publications 2016), both pamphlet collections.

The Horse-Washing Waterfall won a prize in the Poetry Space competition in 2018.

I want to express my gratitude to Erwin Schneider, my husband, for all the help he gives me so that I have space to write. I also want to thank Dilys Wood for her endless support of my work, her useful comments on long poems and publishing this book. Particular thanks are due to Anne Stewart for her work in laying out and proof-reading the text, also to Martin Parker for his cover design and production work.

I also want to thank Caroline Price for her belief in my work and in-depth comments on complex and problematic poems, in addition Mimi Khalvati for insightful feedback and the N7 group. I am grateful to Les Murray who was enthusiastic about my work and published me often in the Australian journal *Quadrant* for over twenty-five years. I much miss this extraordinary poet and his amazing postcards. Warm thanks too to my publisher, Adele Ward, for her interest and support. I am ever grateful to my previous poetry publishers, who are also friends, Stephen Stuart-Smith of Enitharmon Press and John Killick, publisher of Littlewood Press which he ran for several years. Finally, I want to thank artists Robert Aldous and Chris Holley for the inspiration their work has given me.

Previous Titles

Poetry
Fistful of Yellow Hope, Littlewood Press 1984
Cat Therapy, Littlewood Press 1986
Cathedral of Birds, Littlewood/Giant Steps 1988
Opening the Ice, with Ann Dancy, Smith|Doorstop 1990
Crossing Point, Littlewood Press 1991
Exits, Enitharmon 1991
The Panic Bird, Enitharmon 1998
Insisting on Yellow: New and Selected Poems, Enitharmon 2000
Multiplying the Moon, Enitharmon 2004
Becoming, Second Light Publications 2007
Circling the Core, Enitharmon 2008
What Women Want, Second Light Publications 2012
The Door to Colour, Enitharmon 2014
Persephone in Finsbury Park, Second Light Publications 2016
Lifting the Sky, Ward Wood Publishing 2018

Prose
Marigold's Monster, Heinemann 1976
If Only I Could Walk, Heinemann 1977
Will the Real Pete Roberts Stand Up, Heinemann 1978
Writing for Self-Discovery, with John Killick, Element Books 1998
Writing for Self-Discovery, republished Vega 2002
Writing My Way Through Cancer, Jessica Kingsley 2003
Writing Your Self, with John Killick, Continuum International 2009

As Co-Editor
Parents, Enitharmon 2000
Making Worlds, Headland 2003
Four Caves of The Heart, Second Light Publications 2004
Images of Women, Arrowhead Press 2006
Her Wings of Glass, Second Light Publications 2014

CONTENTS

One

Resurgence

Four days they take to cut down
and pulp the sycamore they labelled *sick*,
four days of ladders, of hurling instructions
to roped men chain-sawing upper branches,
of machine-whirr as the body's ground to dust.
Once, it was a singing tree for starlings,
now, sliced, it's flat, a table-top.

A mean wind from Siberia has blown in
and when night lops off day I hurry to the window
to banish weather with a single swish of curtains
but a burst of luminous red in the park
                                   arrests me.
The stump's on fire, its greedy tongues are licking
air – the beauty is shocking. Rough sleepers
seeking warmth, idlers bent on destruction?

A stark porcupine was sprouting from the circle of trunk
but today I'm sure I'll find the tree's remains
are ash. To my surprise it's only charred
                                   and the spines
are now a crown of spindly branches notched
with buds, sturdy promises of green leaf.
I'm so moved by the resolve to live in this world
my heart rises to the sky as if it's a songbird.

Today

Ten to six and light is ribboning
the rift in my curtains. I peer outside
and behold, a white quilt covers the park!

In the silence I watch two luminous
emerald dots hithering and thithering
on its softness. They're too erratic for bikes,

must be uncooped dogs glorying
in kicking up the pale stuff underpaw
and heedless of the polar bear cold

the wind blew in yesterday. Magical,
the traceries of trees, the dark slit of brook,
the creaseless saffron growing in the sky.

At ten to twelve the morning is snowing
its heart out. Annoyed my body
is past its best, I don't risk a walk,

instead sit down in my workroom
and pick a quick route to the orchid house
at Kew on the internet. In seconds I'm gaping

at flowers with speckled tongues, at delicate
apricot and magenta petal-heads nestled
among spears, ferns and lush leaferies

which twine to the glass-paned roof.
As I breathe in the sweet damp air
I seem to see hectic red parrots flapping

and the quiver-wings of a humming bird,
to hear the insistent symphony of tree-frogs
in the rainforest I visited years ago.

A distant voice in the kitchen summons me
downstairs. Trying to forbid the word
endangered, I descend to reality.

Flying

Not only the fork-tailed swallows swooping
and alighting like dancers on a hotel pool
in lakeside Limone one balmy evening;

not only the gulls on Aldeburgh beach shouting
like fishwives, eyes pierced for a chance
to dive and steal fish from the day's catch;

not only that sudden murmuration of starlings,
a whirlwind of dark dots sweeping the air
which stopped me in my tracks on an Orkney island

but also the creature in a see-through sheath.
I wonder what kind of expert fitted it in
as I watch on a screen legs as thin as threads

thrusting against the cocoon's tough sides
to free what seem to be ruffles edged
with black spots until they unfold to reveal

amber wing segments that echo the brilliance
of stained-glass panes. And the wonder is:
this butterfly can navigate as precisely

as an electronic system and it's strong enough
to fly thousands of miles to Mexico to hang
like a leaf all winter, among countless others,

from an oyamel fir high in the mountains.
And the question is: do we have the will,
the wit, to stop destroying its world, our world?

Cushion Moss

The sad paragraphs in the paper offer
no answers but they fade a little once I'm outside
even though there's rain in the air and the sun
silvering naked twigs disappears the moment
I enter the park. I'm in the copse where rooks
are flapping in quarrel as usual, when it stops me
in my tracks: moss cushioning a fallen tree.
The green fabric is so vibrant it's almost luminous.
It awakens grey branches and untidy brambles
emerging from clots of darkness. Hard to believe
this green is natural but no manmade process
could possibly create such soft brilliance.
It's not water-meadow green, not nettle green,
lime green, olive, not glossy laurel,
not intense Lorca green. It's a green spawned
by the damp bedded in rotting logs and deep
leaf mush, a green that's been so mothered
by light it banishes lightlessness, a green
more potent than the science which explains it,
a green which fills my mind, feeds my arteries,
a green that urges: never give up.

Inside Green

For Mimi

Green putting out feelers, green rooted
in earth, intent on living, pushing up,
by May putting on a stunning performance,
urging you to ignore screens, their enticements.

Listen to green and fling open your windows,
your doors to the lawn's massed choirs of grasses,
its clovers and buttercup sopranos eager
to summon up childhood meadows – but don't linger

in the past and miss those small bluish fruits
on the plum trees or the way green's colonized
next door with a field of fescue and brambles
which are climbing the steps to the broken terrace

where buddleia is pressing against its French windows.
Marvel at the elderberry leaping over fences
to the park, then go, go down to the stream adored
by willows, nettle ranks and freckled parsley.

As you gaze at the luxuriance, you'll love green
for its willingness to seed itself in gutters,
drains and cracks, for thriving on crumbling walls
and wherever humans aren't interfering, love it

for concealing the unsightly: tins lost to rust,
empty bottles, straggles of plastic suffocating
coffee cartons. Be still and you'll find yourself
inside green, wedded to its beating heart.

Askew

All night heat has pressed itself against me
like a tiresome lover who ignores refusal
And now I awaken from muddled sleep to light

pushing through the geometry of open window
I created by pinning the curtain back with a chair
to coax coolth indoors. Through the pane

and next door's cross-hatched scaffolding
I examine the world. How peculiar it looks
framed by metal poles and from this angle.

A brash sun is rising but a misshapen moon
is still in the sky as if to utter warning.
I ignore the topsy-turvy of the room, put aside

the paper trumpeting a model in a priceless gown
next to hungry faces, propel myself to the park
to evade the day's heat. A flock of trees

offers moments of cooler air but sycamores
are shedding yellowed leaves, nettles
are drooping, June's succulent green has faded

to the fawn of hay, patches of ground are bald
as the body of an old teddy bear, the footpath
behind the gardens could be a dry riverbed

in Africa. Its cracks are wide enough to trap
a paw, a child's foot. The earth is begging
for someone to dial, demand emergency care.

Tiger

After Henri Rousseau

This is not the tiger which burns bright,
not the silent forest of the night.
The wind rampaging in this tropical forest

is roaring with manic delight as it clenches
hapless trees, heaves trunks,
snaps twigs, twists branches.

Lightning strikes, no majesty here.
The tiger snarls, you can smell its fear
as a heavy branch cracks, falls,

ignites and becomes a vermillion tail
which will spread greedy fire. The sky
blackens. Crouched in the leafery

you watch the beast moving, body
low, fangs bared but not to spring
on prey. Look at its alarmed eyes,

it can't see how to attack noise,
unsteady trunks or maddened leaves.
Suddenly you know this jungle craziness

isn't without but rooted deep within,
know the fear under your corset of bones,
is the tiger, the shocking gleam in its stare.

Becoming Plastic

The morning starts with a tiresome battle to slit
and peel the skin encasing two tubs
of vitamin capsules but it fits as smoothly as a seal's

and I blaze with fury when my fingers can't find
leverage and the sleek containers continue to cling
like inseparable lovers in their see-through wrapping.

Nowadays, everything arrives cosied in plastic:
sultanas, tissues, pears, jumpers, knickers,
the mattress that was tricky to manoeuvre upstairs,

those newly-erected six-storey flats I scanned
yesterday as I walked over Regent's Canal, each
swaddled in the stuff as if it couldn't cope with rain.

In the night I dreamt I struggled through a wild sea
to an island of unrotted rubbish and weakling palms.
A sound of laboured breathing rose from the debris

and I knew plant roots underneath were striving
to survive. A dead grouper stared from a pram
which had lost all its wheels, someone screamed.

I turned, was just in time to see a woman
on a bed with legs parted and a midwife plucking
from her womb a baby sheathed in plastic sheeting.

Grouper: a threatened fish

Trees

To shake off the racket of voices, to escape engine-roar,
brake-squeal, drill – all the ear-splitting noises
human beings fabricate, noise which drowns
rain-patter, birdsong, thought – I go to my suburban park,
make my way into a thicket
                            and in moments
I'm immersed in a silence so deep it releases
the ache in my head. I breathe in the russet sweetness
of long-fallen leaves underneath new buds,
green sycamore layers, frilled orange fungi
clothing a damp stump, hawthorns in snowy
white flower scrambling up earthy slopes, tree roots
in silent conversation underground
                            and it's as if
I'm in the heart of an ancient wood in a distant place.
I press my hand against a beech trunk, whisper
a prayer for forestfuls of trees to heal the planet.

Wind Farms

Skimmed with white first thing, sea and sky
seem inseparable as lovers and the world
looks half asleep until sun begins to silver

the pier's struts. Attuned now, eyes
explore the water. In the distance, so faint
it could be an illusion: a thin-legged flock

with winged heads, a ghostly species
tall as lookout towers, graceful
as long-necked cranes, grazing in silence.

Stare at one close to on land and its height,
the might of its flailing limbs daunts yet excites
as it seizes on the roaring-beast wind

and revels in whirring madly as if to proclaim
it could outdo to a child's plastic windmill
and has enough force to generate electricity.

Praise be for these magnificent birds,
let them inhabit sea, island and ocean,
let them multiply on hilltops and thrive in deserts

as they commandeer hot sandstorm winds
and glory as mile upon mile of lifeless ground
gives birth to the green of grass and tree.

Thrust

For Simon

Often, I daydream of travelling below
grassy banks to the darkness underground
and trapping the moment when a nothing becomes

a something, the moment when a seedling thrusts
into a world of green and blue music,
the makings inside it of sap to feed leaves

and a swan-white flame which will part tips
to reveal a lily lovely as those I saw in a valley
humming with summer below a levada in Madeira.

How insistent life is, even in places
it seems unlikely: the gangly tomato plant
in yellow bud that's sprouted through vents

in a drain on our decrepit terrace, those clumps
of London Pride nifty at rooting in cracks on walls
and against all odds that child who was reared

in a mountain cave in Brazil, roamed
forest wilds inhabited by snake and lynx,
learnt how to scrounge in nearby streets,

at night find crannies to sleep in. Yes,
in spite of hungers, uprootings, in spite of losses
too deep to name, the will to live persists.

The Child: Christina Rickardsson, Never Stop Walking:
A Memoir of Finding Home Across the World

Gold

March, and the tricksy morning has crystallized every
grass blade on lawn and verge. Unfazed as the cows
of my childhood on the loose, a low mist is meandering

down the lightless street but the crescent moon
is a brooch pinned to a whitish sky – how it glints!
Soon the eager sun starts licking up the frost

and there's such a sense of unwrapping, of shedding
winter's layers that even indoors I can feel expectation
stirring inside the park's taut buds. I close my eyes

and see fluid gold pooling. Its kindly warmth trickles
through my body and though my past is beyond
my reach, though the world is knotted with friction, fear,

though hardship, sharper than knife points is rife,
I glimpse Stanley Spencer's newly-awakened dead
emerging from swung-open tombs, bewildered

by daylight and their unstiffening limbs. Suddenly
I'm there, sharing in the glory as they fling their arms
round loved ones, exult in finding they're alive!

Stanley Spencer, The Resurrection, Cookham

Like Small Wishes

four orange-tip butterflies are drifting
across the road and you're surprised to see
the cars, keen carriers of noise and fumes,

are slowing down as if they're feeling sleepy
in the un-British heat. Then, and this is amazing,
the metallic bodies all lift from the tarmac,

their carapaces soften and shrink, their side doors
open, elongate, begin to flutter and the air
fills with tortoiseshell specklings, Adonis blues,

tapestries of dusk and orange. It hasn't rained
yet the sapless verges are now a vibrant green,
concrete frontages have become gardens and each,

crammed with periwinkles, lavenders, buddleias,
is a song of praise. Your feet say goodbye
to the ground, your wings spread, legs unstiffen,

yearfuls of worry fragment, the stricken world
slips off your shoulders and you float to the sky
revelling in a newfound weightlessness.

For Ruth

Two

Let Us

throw open splattered windows
and allow light to stream into rooms,
not shine dimmed to a sullen grey
by a skyful of cloud, not the mean rays
of reason which enumerate facts and faults,
kill compassion and make us hide fears
in cupboard dark, not bright beams
chilled by hatred with more bite
than the east wind –
                    none of these. Let us
open ourselves to today's unstinting light.
It's bringing the warmth of ripe apricot skins,
the happy go lucky orange of marigolds,
the clarity of extra virgin olive oil,
the glory of sun alighting on the waters
of Chania.
            Look, it's kindled the kitchen walls
and awakened cushions in the living room
so let us breathe – let us breathe it in
as it glides up the stairs, smiles
on worn carpets, calms worried beds.
Listen, it sounds like bees murmuring
to the rampant brambles out in the garden.

Summer 2020

The Distance Between Sky and Water

After Robert Aldous The Distance between Sky and Water

Sitting on a sagging, decades-old settee
in a room full of shelves crammed with books
and disordered papers, floor cluttered with chairs,
windows barring the outside, how I ache
for space
           but one step and I'm in an elsewhere.
Breath thumps as I stare black rock –
an implacable precipice rising in steps
high above thought to a shelf
                  which thrusts out
an aggressive chin into the unresisting sky.
It hangs over water inhabited by reed clumps,
water whose depths are unknowable. A relief
that it traps hints of blue and finds a passage
to a sea of colourless calm which merges at last
into an azure seeking lapis lazuli.
                    How small
I am in such immensity, small and frail
as that plant clinging to the cliff but as I stand
transfixed by the distance from sky to water,
self dissolves into the possibilities of space.

Dredging the Moon from the Bottom of the Sea

In memory of Paul Flavell

At the end of the year when threat seems to perch
on every stump, every leafless branch,
when bitterness thorns the air, still your mind

and make your way to the ocean. Grit yourself
against the knifing cold and the shelving beach
even though there's no hint of the moon

and there's nothing else to guide you over the shingle.
Position your arms and as the sky begins to shift
its weighty linen, dive into the sea.

Don't shrink from the wilderness of rocks
and wrecks where shoals of spotted blue skate,
staghorn coral and glass sponges beautiful

as cut crystal vases, are being strangled.
You will find the moon, small as a child's ball.
Gather it in your arms, lift it gently to the surface

and watch it lay a silver path. Now raise it
above your head and in the sky a silvery queen
will emerge from the swirling cloud layers.

She'll reflect on herself in muddy puddles, conjure up
streams of glinting eels in rivers and summon
passageways through every darkness.

*Dredging the moon from the bottom of the sea is an exercise
in qigong, the ancient Chinese practice of breathing, movement
and meditation.*

Knees

Not the soundless blue of a flawless Mediterranean,
not the moon's silver stare,
not even June's green insistence.
What I pull out

from the musty wardrobe of years is shocking pink
and the India inside my head,
its hot paprika reds, saffron, dusty cinnamon.
Clad in these, my knees

which used to take the stairs in their stride but now
balk like bad-tempered mules,
suddenly unlock so I leap down, dizzy as a spring hare
and seconds later I'm racing

to the coast, blood thumping through my body.
On the litter-ridden shore
I grab a broom and sweep, sweep until
the wet sand gleams

and reveals fleshy strands of kelp, crabs skittering
to a pool. Then I sit down
on a patch of shingle, feed on the alluring yellow flowing
from a clump of horned poppies.

Calais Sands

Spreadeagled on my bed, I'm still clothed
in the trapped blackbird's fear, my fear
of feather, wingbeat. In my head
the ceaseless plucking of harp strings
is painful and my body's begging for air
cool enough to breathe but beyond
the open windows the world is sweltering.
Though the bird escaped after a few
interminable minutes its terror belongs
to all the fears swarming through me
like locusts, all the fears circling without.
When I bolt down the stairs hoping
to shake off insanity, the moon,
which queens the night sky and unravels
darknesses, fixes me with a mean
metallic stare. In the kitchen silence
has settled down like a cat, even
the cupboards are placid. I sip water,
dab it on my unhappy skin.
                              The sands
come when I've shuffled back to bed –
or rather I come to the sands: miles
of them. They speak of green slithers
of weed, of lugworms and seep into
a sea of tranquillity that seems beyond
the ruffle of time. And there, perched
on the horizon between the beguiling blue
of hills eased by dusk and what
might be a mediaeval castle,

is half of the sun's gold coin.
Above: a widening river of amber,
below: a glinting pathway over the water
which promises-meanings as it leads
to a scattering of ethereal figures
bent over the shallows. Spellbound,
I let go, drift towards them and, forgetting
they're poissards gathering bait, believe
I've come upon Tchaikovsky's swans
free to be maidens for a few hours.

J.M.W. Turner Calais Sands at Low Water:
Poissards Gathering Bait

Viewing Marianne North

For John

Morro Vellho

I wake locked inside fear but her painting
frees me, its untroubled sky, the violet silence
rising from mountains, that banana flower,
its petals at the point of splitting open to display
a covey of fledgling fruits, a stalk which could be
rope twists but looks as solid as wood.
It hangs like a pendulum to the welter of green
at the foot of the picture. Everything depends
on suspension and balance: the humming birds
pinned by their beaks as they feed avidly
from convolvulus cups, snow-white blooms
latched to twine unwinding against skyblue
and not far below, the aqueduct arches
slung across the gorge's insistent stream.

The Pitcher Plant

Leathery grotesques eager to flaunt themselves,
villains in a grisly fairy story, escapees
from dream? No, fruits of the pitcher plant
which Marianne's allowed to dominate sky
and mountains. The smaller one is lime, pretends
it's a horn with a curving tail. The other's an immense,
reddish shoe with pointed toes and it flaunts
a dainty crimson frill sweet with nectar
round the ankle hole, really a gullet

which lures mice and insects inside to eat.
Once there they drown in hidden liquid, are food
for the captors which seem like tricksters who steal
people's savings but pitchers grow in soil
too poor to feed them and to survive must kill.

Red Parrots

Not crimson, not Christmas card red, not scarlet,
the heads and breasts of these birds but a red
that commands, carries a sense of gold. The blue
of the wings is resplendent too but their beady eyes
are as hard as the tiny fruits on that gum tree
so I expect squawking and feathers flying,
worse – those beaks could draw blood from a stone!
To them noise and quarrel are about mastery,
survival. Below, the mass of lush leafery
scrubby grass and bush stretch to the horizon.
It can't have rained for months, the ground's so dry
the vegetation is ready tinder. At what point
will these parrots sense the world's out of kilter?
Could they cope if their trees were in cinders?

The Papandayan Volcano from Mr Hollé's Tea Plantation

I long to flee my cramped room, its machines
and strewn papers, the cold scrabbling to get in.
I want to be whisked to Mr Hollé's plantation,
waist-deep in one of the plant rows
on that hill and breathe in the scent of leaves

so intensely green they're almost luminous.
Once there I'll gaze at the two peaks black
as panthers fuming whitely into the sky.
Turning, I'll glimpse a family far above me,
tea-pickers, the man in cinnamon
sitting by his basket, his wife and child on foot –
they're little more than specks in the landscape.
How tiny, puny we all are, boasting our skills,
fools who've rushed in to tamper with the planet.

Waterlilies in Chile

No peopled streets, no fumes, no shop fronts
propping the homeless. I have come upon
a lake of tranquillity lined with palm trees,
a dream place where immense lilies beckon.
If I nestled among their petals they'd lull me
into hours of deep untroubled sleep.
Instead I stare, amazed by floating plates
which are emerald and huge, until it dawns:
they're tightly packed leaves and the bulbous vase,
so out of place, is a bud, the pointed nut
bobbing on the many-coloured water,
simply a skin concealing a white flower
with a saffron heart. It's not a mirage, it's real,
this paradise! Who or what created it?

Marianne Paints Mount Fuji

I envy the energy Marianne found
to travel from continent to continent
wearing a weighty black dress that buttoned
to the neck and, bespectacled, sit in hot
exotic places among the flora and fauna
she'd identified, creating songs of colour.
Here, in the land of Hokusai she's depicted
a branch of wisteria arched over a sea
that's been kissed by the setting sun, a sea
on which two tiny figures can be made out
facing each other in a skinny boat.
Beyond it, minute sails are visible and, above
the calm of water fusing with cloud, Fuji
mysterious, sacred, in lavender and white.

Paintings in Marianne North Gallery in Kew Gardens:

The aqueduct of Morro Velho, Brazil.

A new Pitcher Plant from the limestone mountains of Sarawak, Borneo.

View from Collaroy, New South Wales, looking towards the Liverpool Downs.

The Papandayan Volcano, Java, seen from Mr Hollé's tea plantations.

Victoria regia.

Distant View of Mount Fujiyama, Japan, and Wistaria.

Looking at Light

You watch it pounce with obvious delight
on a bottle of water on the table, implanting
a series of intense kisses on the neck,

seizing on the flowers speckling the mat
underneath and multiplying them with delight
in the transparent interior. Another feat:

it's blued the frostbitten park but the sun
will emerge, lay pinkish streamers
on the stiff grass and paleness will disappear

as it douses the air with a sense of gold.
All your rooms will awaken and you'll long
to keep lucidity but it's not long before

crimsons and violets are spilling over the sky
to herald darkness. Yet when day dies
you'll gaze at dazzle-needles which the bottles

on the bathroom window ledge have snatched
from the streetlights, at the electric red
splashed across the panes by a passing car

and for moments illumination will fill you.
Later, you'll wake to a chill nothingness
but you'll find a lemon pool of moon

on the landing carpet, wish you could kneel
and gather it up in your arms, wish
its certainty could show us a way forward.

A Pair of Shoes

One glance at these, ordinary as the actual pair
long dead, and I forget the bricks displayed
on a gallery floor until a cleaner clears them away

for these have a presence which compels
and each is defined as an individual even though
standing side by side they could be taken as twins.

Their toe rims seem to point towards me
as they rise slightly and offer sturdy soles but I'm lured
into the complex planes on their creased uppers

which extend to ankle height where the leathers
of one shoe fall open like wings to reveal
a calf-brown lining, while on the other they curve

to guard legs from rain. I'm mesmerized
by the way both sets of laces travel haphazardly
across the worn uppers like long insect legs,

one set circling strangely before it wanders out
of the painting. And I love it that light, exulting
in the darknesses of this landscape, creates

dabs and streaks of white, pools of pale ochre
and hints of cobalt blue, love it that one shoe
merges into the golds, siennas and umbers

of the surface on which they stand, while the other
is outlined against straw-yellow. I picture him
examining and buying the pair in a flea market,

walking streets in them, positioning each
in front of his easel, the intensity in his room as he lifts
the brush, the sense of endurance the shoes carry.

A Pair of Shoes 1886   Van Gogh

Venice on Ice

For Stephen, after Peter Blake, Venice Fantasies

How strange: an architectural feat in ice floating
across the Grand Canal and no doubt dreaming
itself as cathedral with those pinnacled towers.

The galleon, its companion, is a mystery too –
the furled sails could be outstretched arms
or gannet wings. Even more bizarre, the flotilla

behind them: islets peaked with vanilla snow,
a coracle which thinks it's a meringue laden
with two cherubs and a raft bearing a family.

Irresistible, the feast for eyes on the near bank:
immense icicles descending in beautiful series
of glass organ pipes from the palace balconies.

How bizarre that beyond the ice Venice is bathed
in lemon light the sun's shed on walls, dome
and legs topped by shorts. Is it simply a dream,

the Arctic invasion into this city idling
the afternoon away beneath the lavish blue
or should the dark ship be read as a warning?

What has terrified the mediaeval figures huddled
on the raft, why are the coracle's cherubs too busy
enjoying each other to help them in their plight?

But why dig for meanings? It's always easy
to see signs of disaster. Why not seize the chance
to enter this otherworld, revel in extravagance!

She Is

after Chris Holley Shawl

the swirl of skirt, its many layers,
    the beautiful response of the hillocks
        of buttocks to body when she hollows her spine.

She is rhythm, its compulsion,
    the darkness of night air pulsing
        with passion and her foxy auburn hair announcing

she can't resist the heat of red
    and its play with white as it thrums pathways
        from throat to her thighs, drives that thrust-forward knee

in an unstoppable sweep
    towards an uncooped place of flame
        and crimson. Now comes the moment when she raises

her manton. Watch and you'll see it
    metamorphose into wings, be spellbound
        by the width of its span, the lie of those indigo feathers,

the long whisperings of yellow,
    the weight and weightlessness.
        Though you've caught glimpses of her in the everyday

you know she belongs
    to imagination. Don't struggle to capture
        her fire, open yourself to receive and she will inspire you.

manton : a kind of Spanish shawl

Below

After Henry Moore, Tube Shelter Perspective 1941

Ghosts are they? Two rows of bodies
endless as the tunnel, all lying
with knees raised and heads against the wall:

this could be one of the lowest circles of hell.
It looks as though they're bound in stark white
for funeral but they must be survivors

who want to believe they're safe underground.
Is it you or one of them who fears drowning
in fetid darkness or waking up with wounds

no one can heal? The silence is eerie
as snow, that muffler of sound. Ominous,
the absence of full-blooded colour in this place.

How you ache for the green of grass, the red
of hollyhock. You could bed down with the others
but they might take fright, flee. Somewhere,

a flute, you can just hear it trailing sound
that's clear as the new moon. Now you notice
a lemonish brightness above the pale figures,

watch it hovering. You want it to lighten minds,
allow sleep to flow like a quiet stretch
of river, bring dreams easy as minnows.

Diving In

How limited they are, how heavy-footed
plodding round the pool. Beside them
I'm nimble as Mercury but the tables swivel
when they plunge and those flightless wings
propel swimmers agile as acrobats,
fluid as the glassy green liquid in their tank.
Are they clever birds which fly under water
or fish which have learnt how to walk on land?
Oh for mastery of a cool element
out of reach of the sun's scathing stare!

Suddenly I'm leaping cement walls, breaking
free of clothes, and in my buttonless skin,
I who dread the violence of deep water,
dive in. Nothing matters but escaping
the heat pawing my body, escaping the paper
crushed by my partner's arm yet still croaking
about bewildered immigrants the police
found huddled in a dirty caravan, slaves
forced to toil for their food in Europe's fields.

Nothing matters except this liquid now
and weaving myself between the penguins
easily as an eel. Yet from the muffle above
a nameless something keeps tugging. I rise
against my will to solid ground. No one
sees how hostile it is, no one notices
the diamond drops necklacing my nakedness.
Desolate, I retrieve my scattered garments.

We trail past cockatoos and other exiles
in enclosures meant to make them feel at home.
They wouldn't choose safety if they could plump
for forest. Wordless, we watch a pair of macaws.
One is picking ticks from the glorious tangerine
and turquoise plumage of the other. They kiss
and such tenderness flows through the netting,
I tremble: love can bloom inside a cage,
a derelict wagon, a heap of dung, a desert,
lift you to the sky at anytime, anywhere.

Lake Orta

If you've wrenched yourself from the swaddle of first language
and the home which has always kept you, your feelings safe,
because, exposed to gunfire, it couldn't mother you any longer;

if you've lost someone who mattered and whatever you touch
is devoid of colour and meaning; if you don't believe
you will experience happiness again in the welter we call life,

then you will wander through countless months of wilderness
trying in vain to shake off despair. But at last you may come
upon water – not a muddy pond, a lake of many blues,

a glinting jewel set in a ring of mountains. You will wake
at dawn and as mist rises you will watch an early waiter
feeding swans and listen to the lip-lapping below your window.

At midday the ferryman will appear and row you to the small
enticing island. You will revel in the sun's glitter. The silence
of depthless water will fill you, hope will leap scattering spray.

In the Moment

After Hokusai, Tatekawa In Honjō

Relishing the taste of sweetness in a small
chill hour I turn to the January scene
on the wall calendar. The dark month

instils a sense of doom but in this print
light is cramming a yard. How it revels
in the azure and white of the Tatekawa river –

not a hint of gloom here. Series of poles rise
like pinnacles above the violet-blue hills
and on the ground timber lies pell-mell,

planks jut over the water or rise in stacks.
A labourer, back bent, is perched on one
that towers above docile village roofs.

Blocks of wood he's just hurled are flying
through the air towards his mate below.
I can feel the thrust of the thrower's arms,

the receiver positioning himself to catch –
I'm hooked by the skilled dance of these two men.
Yet in this moment I'm in my night-time kitchen

eating a banana and far from the yard in Japan,
its agile workers, timber intruding on sky –
the moment an artist stopped, began to draw.

The Horse-Washing Waterfall

After Hokusai, In the Horse-Washing Waterfall

Though what I remember is tail after chalky
white tail hanging over sheer
grey rock and, as they become rivers,
wanting to leap from the train to gape
at waters spitting and gasping their way
through the valley,
           Norway vanishes
when I come upon two men with a horse
at the pause in a Hokusai waterfall.
And I can't take my eyes off the scene:
those taut white runlets edged with blue,
their unstoppable descent, the horse
with his head to one side, expression
quizzical, as if he is overseeing
the half-naked men while they scrub,
scrub his back and flank.
           Nearby, the fall
splits again, jams giant fork tines
into the stream below. Nothing is at rest:
sweat is pouring from the labourers' bodies,
the bossy animal keeps swivelling
his neck, spray is scattering dots
over black jags of rock, creating
a night sky that trembles with stars –
even the bushes are thrusting roots
into the mountain's steep sides,
and the omnipotent waters are roaring
in triumph: *movement is everything.*

Cropthorne Church

Silence is the cool as I enter leaving heat outside
like a heavy coat, the floor absorbing my footsteps
as I slip through layers finer than lawn, the scent
of summer flowers intense as the laying on of hands.

Silence is the higgle of mediaeval windows, names
on tablets of stone, each a reminder of transience.
Silence is the birds on an Anglo-Saxon cross,
their carved parrot beaks songless. It is profound.

But why am I here? I'm not a Christian. My belief
is in *the force which rolls through all things*:
the light still reaching us from the early universe,
darkness splitting apart to let morning be born,

rain filling puddle and sea, the will to survive stored
in ovaries, love, minds mastering the beauty
of mathematics, this poignant arch which rises
in the silence beyond the leaning walls of the nave.

Three

In the Comeragh Mountains

For Mark and for my sister, Sheila

Far in and high up, I am released
from the capsule of car into air sharper
than pine needles, air so fresh and thin
I know we are miles from any town. Ahead:
tough reddish grass, mingled with heather,
rising towards ungiving mountain.

                                I gasp
as I'm tugged back six decades to the child
I was who grew up at the edge of moors.
And it matters not that the place was Scotland
not Ireland, the smell I'm doused in is the same
and the gush of long ago, the joy of grasping it,
the grief of losing it, overwhelms me.

                        If I could stay
for a few days I'd re-find the reed beds
which grew on the moor's crest, bog waters
black as coal glinting with suggestion, heads
of white-haired cotton grass maddened
by the wind, the surprise of marsh marigolds,
a curlew's cry piercing the sky – how I wish
I could cancel my evening plane.

                            We're climbing

towards scree and tumblings from walls of rock
when an icy gust shocks my lungs, staunches words –
words count for nothing here. The moors shrink,
diminished to little more than mounds
by this millennia-old terrain which spells out
that clock time is meaningless,
humans' belief in their power, pitiful.

Words

For Caroline

It's stayed, that moment: I was five, sprawled
on carpet soft as our black cat's back
and the grate was alive with luminous orange rocks

which filled the room with a gritty smell of heat.
It was the moment I conquered every word in the book
about the house with a red roof and green door.

Later, the moment on the school bus
when the jumble of letters across a building
by Cardwell Bay suddenly turned into

Mariners Rest and I saw reading unlocked
the world, then the afternoon, when bored
by a boy stumbling over our class book,

I sped on to Maggie Tulliver seizing the scissors.
Her hair falling, her brother's: *Oh my buttons*,
gripped me till Miss Gaul, bitter as her name,

hauled me back to the room and took out the strap,
a snake she kept in her desk. It bit hard into my hand.
I didn't cry – the story was stamped in my mind.

*

For twenty-eight years Muris lived
in a silent languageless world, clapped hands
to ears if it was invaded by an unnerving bang.

The gestures he and his family exchanged only
they understood but I knew he'd decoded
the five sets of shapes on the slips of paper

I'd showed him at sessions when, intent as a cat
on a mouse, he matched each correctly
with its image. In my head I proclaimed his success

in showers of fireworks. Before long he saw
words said more if he joined them together
and I fell in love with signs for deepening meaning:

Grow: the hand facing skywards and rising
a little with the upward fingers bunched; *tree*:
elbow to wrist held up become a trunk,

spread fingers, the branches; *giraffe*: fingers
topping the trunk with *animal*. Signs surfaced
in my dreams, words took on another dimension.

*

I don't want to hear words misused, their mouths
so pulled out of shape by ranting politicians
and other tricksters they betray their meanings.

I want words which are unencumbered, free
as the sheep which wander for miles on fell sides,
not fabrications easy as eiderdowns

that prettify lies. I want tough words:
scrub, bristle, chisel, ferret; words
passionate as those Keats wrote after hearing

the nightingale; thoughtful words, the fruit
of solitary meditation in the quiet of a room
at night or observation from a train window;

words ghostly as the moon swaddled in mist,
delicate as the pink petals of herb robert,
the stalwart words the Anglo-Saxons used.

I want words that plunge me into elsewheres:
Hopkins' *gash gold vermillion*, words
which hint at meanings that lie beyond their reach.

The signs: Paget Gorman system

Anne's Words

In memory of Anne Watson

You loved words, learnt other languages,
could converse in German, French and Russian, read
their literatures but rarely used your own tongue

to utter your inner feelings. Just once,
all those years ago when we were girls
and in summer walked across the South Downs

where larks sang wordlessly high in the blue,
as we lazed in long grass by Stoke Clump
you talked in a low key but convinced about life

and quietened my uncertainty. We both left Sussex
but you returned and despite your busy life
often walked across the Downs alone:

traversed the broad-backed Trundle and climbed
the chalky path to the tumuli on Bow Hill.
I've made do with a wild slope in my London park,

missed the Downs and my childhood moors.
Though we met over the decades you said little
about illness. When you left words on my phone

saying you were well after an operation, would call
after your holiday, I should have phoned, not written,
Now, you're wordless and I'm overcome with grief.

Bicycle

For Jennifer

You had only to mount it and, with the sun
in full swing, the day was a road unrolling
before you, only to mount and its eager wheels

commandeered your legs, a silver juice gushed
into your body and in seconds you were sailing
through Brandy Hole Lane, its darknesses,

its sudden pools of light hung with trees
and pigeon cooing. Away from mother, all
the frictions which wired home, the day unrolled

before you. In minutes you were tackling the Downs,
passing cows munching and Roland's Tower
solitary in a field, its empty eyeholes

rising into the blue where a lark was singing
its heart out. Oh, you were handlebars and pedals,
Hermes wing-sandalled! At the highest point:

Harting Hill cloaked in beeches, the moment
when you glimpsed the world's quilt of mustards
and greens, its toy sheep, scribbled hedges,

handfuls of roofs below. Clutching the brakes
you gingerly rounded the scarp's hairpin bend,
then flowed, weightless, down past Harting's

black and white hollyhocked cottages,
and on, on to Liss and a day of talking
to Jennifer about books, life and everything,

uncaring that going home you'd have to plod
back up the chalk hill on foot. Fifty years
and more have passed since those long rides

yet last night sleepless in bed with a heavy cold,
sneeze after sneeze angering your throat's dry slope,
fearful your voice would be snuffed,

you somehow re-mounted the bike and, limbs
easy as a dancer's, made your wheels
glide over the Downs until day unfolded.

The Real Mrs Beeton

Heaving her enormous bulk onto a bookshelf high
above my bed, pushing until she was out of sight,
took all my strength and it didn't dislodge her from my mind.

But I rebelled against the weight of her disapproval,
shut myself away every morning in that small room
of my own, the room which is me, to let imagination

run wild as brambles and grasses in an untended garden,
coaxed visions into scribblings on paper until desk
and floor were littered, until unblinking as owl eyes,

words stared from my screen. Of course, the moment
I emerged I came face to face with her large a life
on the landing. For years this matron, large-bosomed

and with a voluminous knowledge gathered from decades
of managing a household, followed me around tutting
because I hadn't blanched or basted, couldn't pluck a duck.

She snorted at unruly children sliding down the stairs,
at dust rollicking along skirting boards, rounded on me
for failing to keep a properly stocked linen cupboard.

Then the day I found out this paragon was Isabella Beeton,
a young woman who instead of devoting her life to home
and family like other Victorian wives, travelled by train

with her publisher husband to his London office, wrote
books fat with information – mostly magpied from other books –
about household management, became a money-spinner,

an authority for later generations. I also learnt she'd suffered
several miscarriages, bore two children who died in infancy,
two who survived, died herself after the second –

thanks to Mr Beeton's syphilis. Yet for years books
in her name continued to appear. The matron's ghost
still persists in my mind but what troubles me is Isabella.

For all the thousands of pages this woman produced
in her short life, the *real Mrs Beeton* didn't leave
a single word about what she thought, felt, endured.

The Model

Only a sepia photo but at once I'm in his studio
and breathing in the exotic: those harem pants
which grace her reclining body, the roses by the couch

with drapes positioned to seduce. It's the intensity
in her eyes which hooks me – they reveal such longing
to speak but she knows she must stuff her feelings

into the cavern of self as centuries of women
have done, meek, unfulfilled women. Sometimes
I see them standing limply in corners of rooms,

catch a whiff of the suffocation they endured,
of their airless parlours, vague maladies, depressions.
Among them: my ill-husbanded grandmother

who found some solace in playing her piano,
my musical mother pursed with dissatisfaction.
And I can't stop it, I'm fifty again, my father

is booming on the phone: 'You are secondary!'
I'm crushed even though I'm in another life
but he fades when *they* appear – all the women

who are still hijacked for use in bed, for producing
sons, cooking, cleaning. When will they reject
voicelessness, become *primary* like men?

The Need for Frankenstein

1

Whenever I close my eyes I'm pulled towards it,
a place where mist clears and nothing is visible
from the prow except turbulent fields of ice

which stretch to the horizon. Water, trapped,
can't lap against the wooden body of the ship –
even the grey-white silence feels weighty.

In the distance I glimpse a giant man-shape
driving a carriage across the white desert.
It quickly disappears into pale nothingness.

She's pursuing me too, the girl of nineteen,
an unmarried mother, who first had this vision.
Maybe she half-remembered hiding by the settee

as a child and drinking in the words the poet read out
about a mariner who shot an albatross in a place
of *mist and snow* where ice was *mast high.*

Is it possible to pin down the source of visions
so intense they fix themselves in our bodies
and minds, seem more alive than the everyday:

a face so full of love the viewer could weep,
the perfect apple which vanishes when plucked,
a mystery-shape that unnerves as it hurtles over ice?

A June evening but the sun wasn't dazzling the lake,
rain was slashing the windows with demonic force
as yet again electric storms imprisoned them

and the fire's warmth couldn't defeat the chill
in the room. When Mary looked outside it seemed
as if the Villa Diodati was hanging in a nothingness:

murk had blotted the water below and the snowy
mountains which towered above the villa were invisible
unless lightning struck and for a few moments

they appeared eerily bright as thunder tumbled.
After the lamps were lit Byron entertained the party
with ghost stories he read out from a book and she sat

spellbound by the scene of a faithless lover clasping
the bride he's taken only to discover he's holding
in his arms the lover he abandoned, now cold

and motionless as marble. Did a frisson pass
through Mary – a flicker of recognition that Percy
left his wife when he fell in love with her?

As he finished the tale of a man cursed to bestow
the kiss of death lightning flashed and Byron slammed
down the book, announced they needed something new

and terrible so each of them would write a story.
Did she glance at her lover, remembering
his wild excitement last night when he described

an electric charge forcing a vermicelli strand
to move as though it was alive and how he exulted
in the blasphemous idea of creating human life?

The poet quoted in first section: Coleridge
Mary Shelley conceived the idea for the novel, Frankenstein
after this evening at the Villa Diodati

Three Women on a Beach

After Peggy Somerville

Look, how the sea's ultramarines have crept
into the stripes of deckchairs and how the shore's
pale apricot has delighted an umbrella
that's chatting to its neighbour while it shades
two of the three hatted heads.

       I wish they'd turn –
I long to see the faces of the women
inhabiting those now-dated clothes. They won't.
The three seem intent on the blues and violets
scampering across water and sky.

       Nearby, a girl
who's almost me, has shed socks and shoes,
stands lovely in bare legs, adoring the sun.
The women have unfastened nothing.

       It's 1965 –
soon women's lib will be alive and kicking;
computers are still clunky, fear of climate change
is in its infancy, smartphones and frequent
terrorist killings, are yet to come.

       The three
have an air of calm but I wonder if resentment
about abruptly-ended careers or other emotions
are festering in their minds.

       Maybe one is grieving
for a stillborn child, another finding comfort

in a secret affair although she detests the guilt
and the third is taking refuge in dreams
yet they only exchange nothings without a whisper
of selves.

Perhaps all they feel though
is gratitude for the lulling voice of the waves
as they push in and out, for the seagulls wheeling
high overhead piercing the sky with cries,
and the sun that seems to spell permanence.

Lights

After Georgia O'Keeffe, New York Street with Moon

Up here it's easy to dismiss the ground
where many, struggling with bags full
of misery, have lost their way and nowhere to go.

Up here those self-important blocks
seem to be what matters. You watch them
striving to claim what remains of the sky

but they're competing with three circles potent
as animal eyes in the dark and they lose out
to the lowest – a traffic light's red pupil.

You can feel it boring into your interior
as if to prise out your thoughts, suspect
it finds satisfaction in causing stoppages

with its air of an immigration official who revels
in regulations and never considers need
as he weighs up granting or refusing asylum.

The street light poised above it seems
to be more sympathetic. Its lemonish halo
has drawn in the maroon of the nearest building

but you don't trust its over-bright heart.
As for the moon slotted into a snowy cloud
in the baby-blue sky, it illumines everything.

Sadly, it's too far away from the ground
to unravel all the strands of suffering below
so you must set to and hack a path yourself.

Room

A place that keeps belongings safe,
that shelters you from outside, its unclean air,
its gusts of ear-splitting music, the shove
of rush hour, its packs of pale faces
and the tousled man on the train who pulls
worn shoes from a bag, puts on a pair,
clacks his heels for a half a minute,
then pleads with passengers for money;

a place to sit savouring thoughts
and feelings, once a place you longed
to escape from – that chill dining room
where your parents' anger with each other
erupted over meals until their words
and silences infected every mouthful,
tangled with the trees outside and hammered
on your head until you felt it would break;

a place to shrug off the past if it slips
out of the filing cabinet, to fill with colour:
a silver elephant on a red cushion and the purple
of aubergines; a place to jot sudden ideas.
But what of those with no room, not even
a bed, a shelf to call their own – that man,
on the train, his ludicrous dance, his body
unwashed, his hopeless life in his bag?

Homeless

Months ago, but I can't shift him, a slip of a boy,
not more than sixteen. There he is, still sitting
on the pavement in money-laden Curzon Street,
propped against a lamppost near an upmarket
Tesco Express. His only possessions appear to be
his sleeping bag and a paper cup.
                              I don't suppose
he's noticed the mansion up the road, for centuries
home to the aristocracy, now a grand embassy.
Railings obscure its lawns and guards armed
with rifles are on duty by the gates which are electronic
of course.
              As yet he seems untouched by sleeping rough.
Nearby, leather-bound volumes and silver cutlery
in an open canteen beckon from a window. Even
the Caffè Nero looks posh and he's as out of place
as those gates would be in a housing estate.

Mist edges in as the autumn afternoon sinks
and though there's a sense of red and ochre leaves
winter is hovering in the wings.
                              At the cinema we see
a film about a widower with a heart condition
who becomes homeless because he can't, won't,
jump through bureaucratic hoops. When we leave
diners are feasting in restaurants where a market
was once held –

the lad's in the same spot.
I buy him a sandwich in Tesco. Surprised, his face
breaks into a smile and he grasps my hand
in thanks. I smile too but I'm pierced by shame
sharp as the spikes on the embassy's railings.

August in Arnos Grove

Determined, I suppose, to lap the holiday sun,
he's made his pitch the post box by Sainsburys,
is patting his sad-eyed collie that's a hotchpotch

of a handful of breeds. The dog's in good nick
unlike his master who's flabby and somehow hollow,
refuses the sandwich I offer but asks for milk.

An aged so-and-so I sometimes pass
in the street, who always asks: *are you twenty-one,
beautiful?*, appears from nowhere, butts in

like a patronizing child: *say thank-you,*
then drifts away. The milk makes my fingers
so cold I picture them falling off as I wait

in the tiresome queue to pay. Outside, he puts
the milk in an elderly holdall, wants to chat.
I nod and nod but ceaseless heavy traffic

is blundering down the road and I only catch
the odd word, notice he has no teeth, guess
he's younger than he looks. When I go he waves.

Flowers spilling from the florist shop greet me
with crimson and yellow laughter, the pink mouths
of watermelon beckon from the minimarket,

at the café's pavement tables they're all gorging
on sun but I'm worrying if the milk will go sour
and how long he can stave off the dark.

Four

Siege and Symphony

1

Leningrad 22nd June 1941

A summery morning and Dmitri Shostakovich
basks in the peaceful warmth as if he's in Arcadia's
pastoral bliss until he switches on the radio.
He is appalled then to hear Molotov announce
Hitler has invaded Russia, feels the world
is falling apart. Of course, he's been living
on the edge for some time and, nervous as a mouse
that scuttles into its hole before the cat
is close enough to pounce, he's been careful
to toe the line, withdrawn the *Fourth Symphony*
though he's kept it hidden in a drawer, and now
only writes music to fit state requirements.
He'll never forget the shock of finding himself
on a precipice staring down at the underworld
that evening five years ago when Stalin
came to see *Lady Macbeth*: how he shuddered
each time the brass and percussion were fortissimo
and at his loud laughter at the love-making scene,
even worse was the terror of bowing to the Leader.
What a warning that circumspection is crucial
day and night. It grieves Dmitri that everyone
has lost someone dear, that crying has to be
in secret in the dark of bed under a blanket.
At times he feels he's suffocating. But on this day
of consternation it occurs to him that the warmonger,
a killer from elsewhere, has given him a reason

to release themes he's penned in his mind and write
music the Leader and his underlings will applaud.

2

Leningrad 22nd June 1941

This June morning Yelena Skryabina is hurrying
through her typing, thoughts dancing ahead
to a day out in the country with little Yuri.

By the open window she breathes in the cool,
a cool which smells of newly-laundered air,
a cool which strokes her bare legs but her happiness

collapses like a punctured balloon when her husband
phones from his factory and, prickly as a hedgehog,
tells her to stay at home and listen to the radio.

At noon she hears Molotov's speech, it's halting
as if he's out of breath. Now, the day,
the future seems weighty as a sack of potatoes.

Outside, sunlight presses hard on her head
and she's jostled by crowds elbowing into shops
to buy anything they can lay their hands on.

Seized by the panic, she joins in the rush
to withdraw roubles from the bank but clamouring
at clerks is useless – there's no money left.

In the unbearable heat someone faints,
people swear. At last evening soothes
the air and everything becomes strangely still.

Gourock, Scotland 1941

June 1941, I am five and war
means great grey ships with funnels
moving slowly as slugs on the waters of the Clyde
below our house, stern voices my parents
listen to on the crackling wireless and something
which is happening far away in London
called 'bombed out' so it isn't until
I start going to school at the Greenock Academy,
a place where teachers hit children with a strap
and I try to hide from gigantic boys fighting
in the playground, from the red-faced cook
who rules the canteen and yells at me as she lifts
her ladle, that I begin to understand living in fear.

Leningrad July – September 1941

Once he's arranged a selection of popular tunes
for performance to troops, Dmitri forgets the heat
of July and plunges into in his seventh symphony.

Oblivious to air raids and the tension in the city,
he works with an intensity he's not experienced before.
One day he summons Isaak, his secretary and friend,

rushes to the piano and plays the opening pages
with emotion he rarely shows. When he stops neither
can speak for several minutes. All August

the first movement possesses him and he's deep
into the second on September the 8th, the day
the city is besieged. A week later he surfaces

to speak on radio, delights the authorities
by telling listeners he's writing a new symphony
which proves that life is carrying on as normal.

September 17th: in the room ruled
by his piano, solid furniture, cigarette smoke
and his desk laden with manuscript sheets,

he plays to friends the parts he's finished.
Ignoring the thuds of bombs, they listen spellbound
as he draws out the nuances of orchestral colour.

Sirens wail as he finishes the first movement
so he leaves to hurry his family to a shelter. Anxiety
mounts but he reappears, continues. 'The music

made a colossal impression,' one friend writes,
not daring to say it encompasses meanings
which travel far beyond Hitler's war.

5

Leningrad 1941, September 8th

For once this September evening Lena Mukhina
isn't thinking about Vova, who's in her class,
and if he likes her. While she's eating with Mama
gunfire begins and in moments the din's so loud
it sounds as though the sky is falling down.
In the bolt to the bomb shelter people scatter

down the steps from their flats like spilled peas.
After the all-clear she stares at smoke swirling
and people tearing down the street as if
to escape an erupting volcano. Passers-by
warn a chemical factory's on fire. At home
she slides into bed in her clothes, aware
she'll be summoned by the siren. No surprise
that her diary entry doesn't mention Vova.

That evening Lazarev is surprised to see sparkling
tracer bullets and puffs of smoke emerging
in the strips of sky between the city's roofs.
Alarmed, he hurries on to his cousin's flat.
From the second-floor balcony, he stares at a vast
spherical cloud rising above the canal.
Partly black and partly blindingly white,
it fills the sky. Watching the setting sun
turn it bronze, he finds it hard to believe
that such a spectacle of stunning beauty is fire,
has no idea that oil storage tanks,
a creamery and the warehouses holding supplies
of food for the city will go up in flames that night.

6

London 2016

A lustreless April day. In my workroom
I select Shostakovich on YouTube.
His seventh symphony begins: mournful notes
descending ladders. The snare drum whispers
but grows insistent as more and more sections

of the orchestra are enlisted and the wind instruments'
syncopated hop becomes cocky.
Unstoppable feet are marching into my room.
They belong to minds which a tyrant has drained
of compassion but I can't resist the stomping boots.
They overwhelm papers, screen, desk, walls.
Chaos till the clash of cymbals topples everything.
A silence. From the debris a flute's voice rises.
It's forlorn as a fallen bird, as the faces of packs
of people stripped of hope. There's no weeping
but grey despair's passing through the orchestra.
It's heartbreaking. Sound flickers out.

7

Leningrad – outskirts of Moscow 1941

October and the air bites hard as Dmitri,
carrying Maxim who's three, clambers onto
the military plane followed by wife and daughter.

In spite of his plea to stay, the authorities
ordered him to leave and with essentials only. On board
he's told they're not to sit on the floor or the boxes

so they crouch on their cases in the cramped space.
From under the plane's transparent hood a sniper
is scanning the sky. Moments before lurch off

he looks down, says curtly: 'If I wave my hand
you must all lie on the floor.' Excited by the flight,
Maxim points at the explosions of light. It's dark

as death when at last the plane bumps down
in a clearing in woods near Moscow and the family
is led to a hut for the night. At the edge of sleep

Dmitri is soothed by the damp smell of leaves
but anxiety about his unfinished symphony tugs him.
He fumbles in his case for the score, takes it out.

8

Leningrad 1941

November 16th and the shops in Leningrad
are stripped of food, the restaurants silent as graves.
Rations are reduced, the bread made of sawdust

and cottonseed is a ghost of its former self.
Lena Mukhina eats her meagre consignment
before school, supper is a miserable soup

with a single ingredient: oily meat jelly.
'There's always a gnawing feeling in my stomach,'
she writes, then decides they can just cope

but five days later on her seventeenth birthday
when there's nothing for supper and Mama's still at work
she lets go of her weighty bundle of feelings

and words spill into her diary: 'I'd give anything
to fill my stomach. When will we feel full?
We've been eating liquid slush for more

than a month already.' The next day chocolate
is doled out with bread and as if a blind
has been pulled up, Lena's despair

lifts. 'It's the kind of chocolate you dream about,
real English chocolate – creamy, fragrant,
beautiful' but she scolds herself for pigging

a whole bar and forgetting there's more to life
than food, forgetting factories and cinemas are open,
shrugs off the fact that there's only firewood

or whatever burns slowly for fuel, that people
are so underfed they're as thin as pins and rarely
bother to drag to a shelter during a raid.

9

London 2016

A mean December morning, the wind bullies me
when I open the back door and at once Leningrad
is in my head. I see the city as a sick body
clothed in dirty snow, think of Lena
in the flat on nights when the electricity's off,
without heat or radio, shawled in a blanket,
writing her diary in bed by candlelight.
No way to stop the merciless cold
sinking its teeth in deeper if the belly's empty.
Lifting the lid of the squirrel-nibbled bin
outside our back door, I stoop to tip
lumps of stale bread over flaccid cabbage
and rotting apples, try not to shiver.

10

Kuibyshev December 1941 – January 1942

January and Dmitri's forgotten the seven days
and seven nights as they journeyed to Kuibyshev
crammed in a carriage with Bolshoi dancers, forgotten

how in the noise, confusion and clouds of steam
on Moscow's Kazan station, their suitcases
with his white-hot manuscript were left on the platform,

and how panic that gripped him in its vice till he learnt
they were safe, forgotten the camping in a classroom
after they arrived and the one room assigned

to the family which at first felt like living in paradise,
then a cell where he was shut off from music,
forgotten that the grand piano presented to him

was a bulky white elephant until it had a room
to itself in the flat they were given. Here, he settles
but it's only when he knows Hitler's attack on Moscow

is failing that his energy flows again like sap
through new leaves. At once he hurls himself
into scoring the final movement, his concentration

so intense it holds off the ferocity of December.
At last the night when, taut as a violin string,
he starts playing the finished symphony to friends.

The first movement is building up when the phone
cuts in. Its tone is insistent and Samosud, who lives
in the flat underneath, begs to come up and listen.

The visitor is motionless, still inside the music
when the playing stops so he's unaware of the rush
to heap praise until he notices Dmitri is leaning

against the piano as if it's a supportive friend,
his face like a fearful cat's. Smiling, he crosses
the room, tells the composer with total certainty

his symphony will be performed all over the world,
announces: 'I start rehearsals tomorrow.' Dmitri
cradles the score, then entrusts it to the conductor.

11

Leningrad 1942

February: it's freezing and thousands are still dying.
Bodies lie hard as rocks in the snow
until relatives stoke up the strength to tow them
to a morgue. Lena writes a single sentence
on the 8th in the middle of a page: 'Mama died
last night, I am alone.' On the 11th, dazed
by loneliness, she asks the voiceless diary:
'Who will guide me now?' On the 13th
incomprehension, rage and grief seize her
but she lights the big stove, cooks, copes.

Death crouches in corners and doorways
but by the skin of their teeth many contrive
to stay alive. At the Architects' Institute
the blueprint work is the best medicine
they could have been prescribed. Canny scholar,
Aleksandr Boldyrev, a Persianist who often quarrels

with his wife, lines up for a meal in the canteens
of all the places he lectures. At night he packs
his stove with chopped furniture and picture frames,
coaxes it into feeding him red warmth,
then lies beside it on the sofa and travels far
from the siege in books: *Great Expectations*,
a delight apart from the graphic reminders of food,
The Good Companions, light-drenched *Kim* –
a gift from heaven. He sorts the shrinking stock
of furniture and his books into: keep; sell; burn.

12

London 2017

March and in the park the willows are in full leaf
yet even here I'm haunted by huddles of citizens
bundled up in black, queueing with pails

in the troubled snow for water from a stand pipe.
I want to believe such a destructive siege
couldn't happen again but at once Aleppo's in my head:

leafy boulevards mashed into a hell
of broken masonry, blank windows and wires;
children with grazed, dirt-smeared faces

creased in misery or numbed by trauma; Aleppo
fought over for four years and, thanks
to iPhones always visible, audible to the world;

Aleppo which we watched as doctors begged for drugs
and blood to treat the injured, as aid workers
were ambushed. For all our clever technologies

we couldn't save these people, their homes,
the sumptuous hotels, the ancient Citadel, the Souk
crammed with spices, copperware and carpets

displayed to show the glory of their patterns. Even
the jasmine and honeysuckle which scented the air
were crushed by falling buildings, lost to dust.

13

Kuibyshev 1942

March 5th and Dmitri, aware that dozens
of musicians and officials are coming to Kuibyshev
to attend the first performance of his new symphony,
is sick with fear it will be a flop. All day
he flaps from room to room like a worried hen,
clucks inanities to family and friends.
Does he unwind when he hears *bravos* rising
above the columns or does he only relax
when he reads Pravda's song of praise that ends
Hitler doesn't scare Shostakovich?
He's no idea little Maxim keeps hearing
the sound of the snare drum growing louder
and louder and for many nights cries himself
to sleep, terrified the Germans are coming to get him.
The *patriotic symphony* is a triumph at its premiere
in Moscow. Afterwards its score is microfilmed
and sent secretly to the rest of the world in a tin.

Leningrad February - April 1942

By February only one orchestra is left
in the maimed city: the Radio Symphony.
They last performed in the freezing blue and white

of the Philharmonic Hall in December. Many players
have died but Eliasberg scrounges others
from the military and the city, determined to rehearse

popular Tchaikovsky for a concert so he calls
a meeting. Only sixteen succeed in turning up
and half of these have struggled out of sick beds,

can hardly climb the stone steps to the room
they've been assigned. Ksenia Mateus, the oboist
is worried when she sees some have lice crawling

on their collars, some soot-smeared faces.
Conductor and musicians are too weak to play
for long but all are rewarded with a meal. Cheered,

they take the unexpected treasure to their families.
Propped up by raised rations, they manage
to cope with longer rehearsals. On April 5th

every tier in the baroque Alexandrinsky
is sardine-packed. Karl Eliasberg
appears, starched and in tails, but when he lifts

the baton his hands begin to shake. To Ksenia
he looks like a bird that's just been shot
and is about to plummet. Then his hands still.

Leningrad July-August 1942

In July the precious score arrives from Sweden
by plane. The players' parts are hastily copied,
rehearsals begin but Shostakovich's symphony
asks too much of the depleted orchestra
and air raid sirens cause interruptions.
Undaunted, Eliasberg lengthens rehearsals,
punishes latecomers and ignores the mutters
of mutiny he often senses behind his back.
Then the day when black jackets, bow ties
and dark dresses are doled out. They hurriedly
try them on and Ksenia, who misses nothing,
notes they all look like coat hangers.

August 9th. It's the day! To ward off attacks
General Govorov mounts operation *squall*
against the enemy. At 6pm a recorded address
by Eliasberg is broadcast. His voice is pent:
'Tonight's performance of the Seventh symphony
by our outstanding citizen is witness to our spirit...'

7.30 and the Philharmonic is packed
with grandees and civilians wearing best clothes
they'd forgotten existed. Outside, the huge crowd
waiting to listen on loudspeakers, is keyed up.
The orchestra files in, its members trying conceal
their anxiety. The chandeliers above the stage
are suddenly spheres of light, glitter, dream.
The hall falls quiet, Karl Eliasberg
bows: the Leningrad Symphony begins.

Many in the audience are so moved they weep.
Olga Kvade can't stop thinking of her Papa,
how much she misses him, the Chopin waltzes
he'd taught her to play. She feels as if he's sitting
beside her, tells herself she mustn't cry
but think how proud she is of the orchestra
for ignoring the shelling. Many Germans hear
the symphony too – the loudspeakers carry it
through the chill air to no-man's land.

When the final movement starts, as if
they are one body, the whole audience stands.
It is evident some of the players are so fatigued
they're faltering but the listeners will them on,
an electric tension binds them all together
At the end: utter silence, then a storm of clapping.
The joy is almost unbearable. A young girl
runs up to the podium, blushes as she offers
dazed Eliasberg a bunch of fresh flowers
from a city garden, flowers that defy the blockade.
Marigolds are they? Blue cornflowers?
In the hall, outside, the ovation goes on and on.

*Details in this poem are drawn from primary sources in the
following books: The Diary of Lena Mukhina, Pan Books,
2016; Leningrad, Tragedy of a City under Siege 1941-4, Anna
Reid, Bloomsbury 2011; Shostakovich, A Life Remembered,
Elizabeth Wilson, Faber and Faber 1994.*